A Kind of Perseverance

MARGARET AVISON

A Kind of Perseverance

THE PASCAL LECTURES
ON CHRISTIANITY
AND THE UNIVERSITY

edited by Stan Dragland and Joan Eichner

The Porcupine's Quill

Library and Archives Canada Cataloguing in Publication

Avison, Margaret, 1918–2007
 A kind of perseverance / Margaret Avison.

Contains two lectures, Misunderstanding is damaging and Understanding is costly, given at University of Waterloo in 1993, as part of the annual Pascal lectures on Christianity and the University.
ISBN 978-0-88984-326-4

 1. Avison, Margaret, 1918–2007 – Religion. 2. Christian life. 3. Church and education. 4. Poets, Canadian (English) – 20th century – Biography. I. Title.

PS8501.V5Z47 2010   C811'.54   C2009-906356-5

Published by The Porcupine's Quill, 68 Main Street, PO Box 160, Erin, Ontario NOB 1TO. http://porcupinesquill.ca

Represented in Canada by the Literary Press Group.
Trade orders are available from University of Toronto Press.

We acknowledge the support of the Ontario Arts Council and the Canada Council for the Arts for our publishing program. The financial support of the Government of Canada through the Book Publishing Industry Development Program is also gratefully acknowledged. Thanks, also, to the Government of Ontario through the Ontario Media Development Corporation's Ontario Book Initiative.

ONTARIO ARTS COUNCIL
CONSEIL DES ARTS DE L'ONTARIO

Canada Council   Conseil des Arts
for the Arts   du Canada

A NOTE ON THE TEXT

This edition of *A Kind of Perseverance* – first published in 1994 by Lancelot Press, Hantsport, Nova Scotia – corrects errors in quotations and in bibliographic information. Some bibliographic information, absent in the previous edition, has been supplied. Editors' annotations in the text and endnotes appear in brackets.

INTRODUCTION

At the 1963 Vancouver Poetry Conference, Margaret Avison's answer
to the question 'What makes a poet's language distinctive?' was: 'It is
saying "I am here and not not-there".' Here in her 1993 Pascal Lectures, she uses the same proposition in a different context, that of a
Christian trying to live out and communicate her faith in a secular
environment: '... if we are *here*, we cannot genuinely be *there* as well.
But we can hope to be "not not-there"' (Lecture 2, p. 39).

'I am here and not not-there', then, describes Margaret's stance
both as a poet and as a Christian. She would often say that it's the
poetry that matters, not the poet; similarly, it's the person of Christ
who matters, not the person talking about Him. She hoped her words
would communicate to the reader/listener without being distorted by
a personal response to her as writer/speaker.

In these lectures, 'Misunderstanding Is Damaging' and 'Understanding Is Costly', Margaret's context is specifically life as a Christian in a secular university. The tension between being 'in the world'
yet 'not of it' meant she must listen to and live with compassion
towards non-believers without compromising her own values, a dual-
ity which could easily lead to misunderstanding and hurt on both
sides.

Interestingly, some titles of Margaret's poetry collections reflect
her aim to hold the eternal and the temporal, the 'I am here but not
not-there', in healthy tension throughout her years as a Christian: *Not
Yet But Still*, *Always Now*, even *No Time* in its double meaning. She
was continually working out her 'own salvation with fear and trem-
bling' (Phil.2:12, NKJV). These lectures give us a rare glimpse into the
process, which is the practice of 'a kind of perseverance'.

JOAN EICHNER

PREFACE TO THE FIRST EDITION (1994)

This little book contains the two lectures delivered as the annual Pascal Lectures on Christianity and the University at the University of Waterloo, Ontario, Canada in March 1993. Blaise Pascal (1623–1662), the seventeenth-century French mathematician and religious philosopher, is remembered today for his establishment (before Newton) of the calculus, and as the author of a book of Christian meditations, the *Pensées*. Members of the University of Waterloo, wishing to establish a forum for the presentation of Christian issues in an academic environment, have chosen to commemorate the life of Pascal by this annual event.

The Pascal Lectures bring to the University of Waterloo outstanding individuals of international reputation who have distinguished themselves in both scholarly endeavour and Christian thought or life. These individuals discourse with the university community on some aspect of the academy: its theories, its research, its leadership role in our society. The speaker is invited to challenge the university to search for truth through personal faith and intellectual inquiry focused on Jesus Christ.

Margaret Avison has twice been honoured with the Governor General's Award for poetry. The first award was for *Winter Sun*, published in 1960; the second, for *No Time*, published in 1989. Betweentimes she testified to having become a Christian on January 4th, 1963. Although she was brought up in a minister's family, she describes herself as having been a rebel on 'a long wilful journey into darkness', preferring her own idea of Jesus as an ethical person to 'the priority, Christ's pervasive presence'. One year earlier, in January of 1962, she had written to Cid Corman, 'There is some corner I have to turn yet, some confronting I have to do – as you would instantly agree, I think, it must come about at the deepest levels in order to find free singing voice.' Then she added, 'Somewhere in this effort, a wrong self-effacement has taken place in me. I can feel the blindfold, the straitjacket – but cannot so far discover where the knots and hooks are to undo them.'

A few months later, she says, someone came and untied the hooks and knots for her, took off the blindfold, and turned on the light. Or, as she says in poetry,

> We didn't know you, Jesus,
> You came out in the night
> And poked around the side streets
> To give us your light.
>
> ('Ps. 80:1', *sunblue*)

The impact on Margaret is everywhere evident in her poetry, as for example in the title poem of *The Dumbfounding* (1966). Of the encounter she says, 'I would not want to have missed what he gave then: the astounding delight of his making himself known at last, sovereign, forgiving, forceful of life.' Her poetry at this point reminds us of so many recording a similar encounter: Francis Thompson in 'The Hound of Heaven', T.S. Eliot in 'Journey of the Magi', S.T. Coleridge in 'The Rime of the Ancient Mariner', e.e. cummings in 'i thank You God for most this amazing', even Shakespeare's Bottom, a weaver transformed into an ass who, discovering himself beloved by Titania, Queen of the air, and singing of 'his most rare vision', is marvelled at by his fellows as 'a very paramour for a sweet voice'.

That same year, Margaret says, 'it became centrally important to me to see that nothing, nothing at all, could be excluded from the total relevance of the person, Jesus.' So in the autumn of 1963 she returned to graduate school at the University of Toronto. There, twenty-three years after having obtained her BA, she began to write her MA thesis on Lord Byron, finding the conversational style of his poetry refreshing (we see echoes of Byron's style in her own poetry now). Yet she soon developed a growing malaise in moving between the church and the secular (especially the university) world.

Much of these two lectures is an exploration of that malaise, leading to the conclusion that it may have begun by her 'rushing too much' in testing undigested truths, such as the truth that 'anywhere with Jesus I can safely go', but was also caused by the counter-

Christian assumptions and standards of the university, as well as by the temptations of her traffic with secular society. One instance she offered, in answer to a student's question at the end of her first lecture, was when a close friend said to her one day in tears, 'But Margaret, that is a lie!' Seeing the cost of this confronting of her by her friend, Miss Avison said, she faced afresh the Truth, the Word, who confronts us to bless. One result of this kind of facing was that she left the university and began to work at Evangel Hall, a Presbyterian inner-city mission. Many of her poems are her records of experiences – her malaise – there.

The malaise never ends, she says: it is how we work out our salvation.

Her comings and goings with the university community continued after she left graduate school at the University of Toronto. Earlier she had worked for the Canadian Institute of International Affairs, then in 1954 had attended the University of Indiana School of Letters. In 1956–57 she took up a Guggenheim Fellowship in Chicago, and in 1972–73 was Writer-in-Residence at the University of Western Ontario. Meanwhile she had published a children's history text, *History of Ontario* (1951), had translated Hungarian poetry for *The Plough and the Pen*, and published *The Research Compendium*, consisting of abstracts of theses from the Toronto School of Social Work. These professional associations with the university were accompanied by formal links through her local church, Knox Presbyterian in Toronto, which has many of the university community among its congregation.

Always she wrote poetry. Some reviewers speak of Margaret Avison's poetry in terms of its sensitivity: 'subtle shadings of emotion', 'deeply religious and vulnerable', 'social concern and moral values fused by religious conviction' are the terms of Michael Gnarowski. Others such as John Kertzer and Michael Higgins point to her use of nature imagery – sun, snow, winter, spring, rain as metaphors for her spirituality – and think of her as a pastoral poet. Still others speak of her poetry's complexity, comparing her to Gerard Manley Hopkins and using such phrases as 'intentionally cryptic' or 'very intellectual' (Milton Wilson and William New). Many speak of her poetry's importance to Canada – 'the most significant book of poetry in Canada since the modern movement got under way,' wrote A.J.M. Smith in 1966 of *The Dumbfounding*. The same sort of tribute was made in 1960 and 1990 by her receiving Governor General's Awards and yet again in 1985 an Order of Canada Medal.

Robert Browning in his poem to Elizabeth, 'One Word More', points out that we eagerly welcome a prose statement from an artist who normally works in the medium of poetry, for we hope thereby to get a better grasp, a more logical, discursive explanation of the truth we have reached for in the ever-enlightening yet ever-elusive words of the poetry. However, this prose of Margaret Avison, as of Milton, Donne, Coleridge, Eliot, is only scarcely disguised poetry once again, and the better for being so, presented as it is with poetic devices rewarding in the dense intensity of its imagery. Yet Browning concludes that we can most wholly apprehend the artist in his primary medium. Miss Avison would seem to agree, for she says:

When he is writing poetry, a person is at his most intense, his most clear-sighted. All his faculties are alert and fused in a single, supreme effort. And the statements he makes at that pressure point of crystallization must be relatively more valid than the conclusions he may form in his more casual, intellectual, self-conscious moments. – *Canadian Forum, XXIV,* June 1944, 67

(Quoted by Jon Kertzer in 'Profiles in Canadian Literature,' 1980)

Nevertheless, we yearn for her prose statements. So she prepares us for Lecture 1, 'Misunderstanding Is Dangerous', by explaining that she is giving us 'ideas in cumulative clusters rather than logical steps'. Here she offers 'propositions' with her buoyant hope and faith that 'by the end they may have filled out and clarified for us'. She gives us all we need for that filling out and clarifying through her own testimony, and in her pointing to the testimony of Newman, Pascal, Maritain; Boethius, Burton, Tillyard; Dryden, Milton, Klein. Above all, to Jesus Christ, a Person who 'is not boring', who, 'seen clearly, can not be rejected'. He is, says Miss Avison, 'God translating himself into the language of our kind of being'.

In Lecture 2 Miss Avison again proposes 'a propositional magnet-ing of ideas' rather than a logical order. Arthur Koestler in *The Act of Creation* helps us understand this kind of writing when he says that 'great scientific discoveries and artistic creations are alike in that both originate in the discovery of hidden analogies.' She offers to the uni-versity students, those capable of 'the panoramic insights peculiar to the young', those with 'that wide-angle lens flooding one with bril-liant pain and comprehension', some propositions. One is the possibil-ity of 'being here as well as not not-there'.

She says that when Christian and counter-Christian face subject matter uncongenial to both, it is the Christian, knowing the inex-haustible Word as companion, who is more likely to develop receptiv-ity. And she observes that in her search there was a long time in which she refused the spiritual food necessary to appease her hunger.

Throughout these two conversations with us, Margaret Avison testifies of the Word by observations about the etymology of words: 'understanding', 'misunderstanding', 'damaging', 'danger' and, espe-cially, 'pain', with which she is intimate. There is a stillness in the energy of her compassion which makes the good tears start, bringing healing to the sufferer with whom she communes. Our privilege has been more than her poetry, more than these poetic-prose talks. Our privilege has been her presence.

JOHN NORTH
Department of English
University of Waterloo

Man's greatness comes from knowing he is wretched....

                    Pascal, Pensée 114

Denying, believing and doubting are to men what running
is to horses.

                    Pensée 505

The Christians' God is a God who makes the soul aware that
He is its sole good: that in Him alone can it find peace; that only
in loving Him can it find joy....

                    Pensée 460

LECTURE ONE:

MISUNDERSTANDING

IS DAMAGING

PREAMBLE TO THE PROPOSITIONS

The 'and' in *Christianity and the University* raises the question: what connection is implied by this connective?

Certainly I cannot pretend to speak for, or to, the University, or for all Christians. I can speak only from a sporadic acquaintance with University campuses, and as a Christian. The ideas are in cumulative clusters, rather than in logical steps. Therefore I would like to start with a few Propositions, hoping that by the end they may have filled out and clarified for us.

PROPOSITIONS

No mortal person has perfect understanding.

A growing person keeps facing misunderstanding, and keeps breaking through. The old is damaged but ahead is new understanding – of self or of another.

Each new perspective can make some further misunderstanding evident.

Do all of us grow? Well, it takes some doing ... risking further damage, facing the danger, not ducking it.

But if the other person is ahead in understanding at point B, you and that other person will probably misunderstand each other at that point! Isn't it odd how difficult we find it to expect that when we 'don't get it', it is a blind spot in us? If someone else claims to see when we don't, we tend to think, 'Oh, they are wrong!' or 'I don't see that; it can't be so.'

Thinking we know, now, is the key danger to confront. Knowing, now, is essential. In other words, the growing process is dangerous, and essential.

MISUNDERSTANDING IS DAMAGING

When the title of this series is 'Christianity and the University', why are my lecture titles about misunderstanding and understanding?

University and Christianity came together, in my own experience, when I returned to graduate school (the fall of my twenty-third year after graduation) and when I became a Christian (January 4th of that same year). It was altogether a watershed year. Day after day, the 'alls' of the Gospel were hitting me. It became centrally important to me to see that nothing, nothing at all, could be excluded from the total relevance of the person, Jesus. Perhaps now, I thought, extra schooling would open out new prospects – and whatever happened, I felt sure, would illuminate something afresh about the Person of Jesus who is everywhere concerned, everywhere Sovereign.

But in graduate school came an unexpected struggle. In a seminar I was assigned a paper on Byron. The part of Byron I narrowed in on was the later work, and I found I was delighting in the new 'voice' he found for his times, his venture out of the literary language into conversational English, his daring interplay with a very ambivalent audience. The tutor read my paper and said it would be a good point of departure for an MA thesis, and we defined the extra focus as the relation of this new voice to a new reading public, as literacy was spreading and newspapers were proliferating. The poem to be dealt with was *Don Juan* – the very title mocked the stand-pat Englishman abroad who insolently anglicized any word or name he chose – hence Byron rhymed Don Juan with 'new one', as he might rhyme Paris with Polaris. It was witty, irreverent, worldly, sophisticated poetry. It was fun to work on. But increasingly I was feeling uneasy.

Certainly I would agree with Cardinal Newman that we cannot deny the particular 'historical literature, which is in occupation of the language, both as a fact, nay, and as a standard for ourselves'. For 'if we think it allowable to know the state of things we live in, and that national characteristic which we share', then, we must take what the literature gives us![1] His own application of this principle came hard, as appears when he speaks of *Paradise Lost* and *The Rise and Fall of the Roman Empire*. Milton and Gibbon were repugnant to him as men:

We may most seriously protest against the spirit ... and the tendency ... in every page of their writings, but there there are, an integral portion of English Literature ... each a proud and rebellious creature of God, each gifted with incomparable gifts....[2]

There are clues to a measure of misunderstanding in this passage from Newman, aren't there? It would be surprising if there were not, given the very different points of view Milton and Gibbon represent, given England's lingering awareness of the regicide and the Commonwealth period, given Newman's political exasperation with the new liberalism of his day. In spite of all this, his conclusions were fair-minded.

My uneasiness was harder to explain. Another twenty-five years have passed since that Byron thesis. I see now that I was rushing too much. I was over-hasty in testing a truth I had not digested myself! In my joyful state of newfound faith, in those graduate school years, I did not confront, indeed scarcely glimpsed, any conflicts or risk of compromise. There is an old chorus that buoyed me up: 'Anywhere with Jesus I can safely go.' What created my growing uneasiness then?

The university, weekdays, and my new church, weekends, were very different societies. They had very different admissions qualifications. The university's made it an intellectually exclusive community, the church's defined it as socially inclusive. On campus the general assumptions and standards were far closer to my pre-conversion way of thinking than I could now fit in with, given my newfound convictions and imperatives. To study (reading receptively as best I could, and assessing in objective terms) seemed valid enough. But working out the implications of my faith then was a beginner's learning to walk. I needed the support of a Bible passage even when I lacked the Biblical context that would give it clarity; and I needed the example and words of church people, even though I felt that if they had known the content of my work-hours they would have had questions about it.

At times I felt like two persons, or two-faced in either context. The commitment to a Christian priority was clear, and genuine. But so was the response to the literature with all the undertow of other values it brought in. I could not deny either.

I am grateful now that *Don Juan* was the fulcrum of this balancing act. Suppose it had been a paper on Donne's sermons, or on Gerard Manley Hopkins, might not the congeniality of the subject matter then have soothed alertness? Might I have felt so secure, both on campus and in Christian circles, that traffic with secular society would grow less and less until it was no threat, and no challenge? Or, given success with a specialty close to my own point of view, might the gradual pressure toward academic advancement, and the increasing need to keep up in one's field, bit by bit have worked with the subtle undertow, and confused priorities unnoticed? One learns either way. Byron and Christianity was my way then.

The uneasiness made me think. There is something in this that I do not understand, I said to myself. And I would be making a dangerous mistake to attempt a quick fix in the dark. The priority, Christ's pervasive presence, was primary, and clear; how that related to these other pulls (pulls that seemed valid and distracting) I did not know.

Then I remembered a lecture given by Maritain at St. Michael's College when I was twenty or so. He spoke on aesthetics. Much of it was over my head, but I vividly remember an exchange during the discussion period at the end. A student asked: 'Dr. Maritain, how do you reconcile the Christian aesthetics you have presented with the poetry of Baudelaire?' After a moment's thought, Maritain smiled and with a little shrug he said: 'But you will never take Baudelaire away from a Frenchman!'

His response was a beautiful example of humility. He was well able to theorize – about stylistic beauty in relation to truth, about ways one learned, through such writing, to listen to someone with very different experiences – and about how love must learn to listen. But he left all that, and signalled simply: That is a good question and I am not satisfied with any answer I might give, at this point.

Acknowledging that I am dissatisfied with my present understanding of a question is consistent with honouring the priority that forced me to raise the question in the first place. Waiting is not unrewarding. And it is altogether different from giving up, or hedging. Resignation would say, 'This may be true for you, and that is true for me, and agreeing to disagree is the best we can hope for.' But resignation is not hope. The university says, 'Whatever is true for you, let us help you learn how things would look if your viewpoint were this writer's, or that historical period's – and you may find it changes you, or opens you to conversations in a new way.' Christianity says, 'Please let us keep communication open, anticipating unexpected new points of contact, daring to trust that one day one of us or both of us will break through to a new understanding.' '[C]ommunication,' after all, 'is not a relation between opinions, but between human beings.'[3] Yes, these approaches may risk new conflict. But alienation and politeness are the deadlier dangers. Clearing up misunderstandings is a long process. And the robin in the egg does not know that the robin's egg is blue.

In a linguistics class once, in Bloomington, Indiana, I was one of several students asked to write phonetic transcriptions on the blackboard – the instructor worked from our samples to clarify what he had been teaching. When he came to my attempt he frowned, and then his face brightened and he said, 'Oh, northern North American colonial.' He read my 'accent' – I did not know that I had one until then, only that the southerners around me spoke with accents.

We are blind to our blind spots in the same way we are deaf to our accents. The perspective of our time on an earlier time is often instructive. For example, the seventeenth century gave us an encyclopedic exploratory medical work, *The Anatomy of Melancholy* by Robert Burton. By today's categories, it would not be called a medical work, for it includes much religious reflection, echoes of a lifetime of reading, and numberless fascinating detours. But it does cover symptoms, therapies, conditions that may cause a disorder, and so on. Do scientists read Robert Burton today? Doctors and medical social workers simply have no time, and even if the pressures of their responsibilities did not make it impossible, would they have the cultural context to pick out useful observations and discard what appear to our precise, specialized times as great swamps of irrelevancy? (Maybe we should have a serious debate, in university circles, about the value of knowing something about everything as against knowing everything about something, especially in the context of the 'holistic' conversation that goes on all around us in our times?)

My examples are so far drawn from English studies. But does not every subject in this world of learning, pursued far enough, lead out into others? Through Tillyard's *Studies in Milton*, I came upon two passages that led, first to philosophy, and then to physics.

Milton makes Adam tell Raphael the story of his creation, of the first motion of his consciousness. Adam's first conscious act was to 'turn his wondering eyes toward heaven'. He then scanned the landscape, found he could name the things he saw, asked the natural objects around him if they could tell 'how came I thus, how here', and, answering his own question, concluded: 'Not of my self; by some great Maker then./In goodness and in power præeminent.'[4]

The poet Dryden, Milton's younger contemporary, wrote a rhymed opera derived from Milton's *Paradise Lost*. In Dryden's text, says Tillyard, 'Adam is discovered "as newly created"....' His first words are:

What am I? from whence? for that I am
I know, because I think....[5]

Philosophy students will recognize the influence. For Dryden, Descartes opened up a new man-centred speculation, replacing the approach of earlier ages, through nature, through the Creation, toward the Creator as centre. Although Milton was a political radical, although he had visited Galileo, although, as foreign secretary, he had wide continental contacts, nevertheless he 'belonged firmly to the pre-scientific age, when philosophy was still a part of theology'.[6] (His convictions endorsed his inherited assumptions.) Whereas the younger Dryden risked a kind of bungee-jump, all the more firmly disciplined because it was so radical, so daring.

Both no doubt failed to understand Adam – both wrote from our after-Eden context. Dryden *was* distorting Milton's poem in his rethinking – putting man, thinking man, at the starting-point. But of course *not* to respond to Descartes at that period, *not* to risk the new assumption, would have been historically impossible for that young man Dryden, almost three centuries ago. For the whole climate of thinking was changing then. To Milton the universe was constructed on the mechanics of Aristotle, and its planetary spheres presupposed 'sublime intelligences' whose hands were always busy keeping the spheres spinning. The Divine Power was, in physics then, everywhere. Before long, though, 'the modern law of inertia, the modern theory of motion … helped to drive the spirits out of the world and opened the way to a universe that ran like a piece of clock-work.'[7]

Seen in a long historical perspective, every position is a correction of another, calling in turn for correction. (A pendulum suggests nothing but the same arc; a spiral suggests value comparisons; I lack the right image for this thought.) The 'new' science of Dryden's day, and of Coleridge's day, is questioned by scientists of our day.

'[T]his modern age … so often overlooks or despises its origins,' says John Read, then professor of chemistry at St. Andrews University in Scotland. He is looking back to those 'true adepts' among the alchemists who were seeking 'material evidence of the truth of a philosophical system'. Such seekers are easily overlooked in 'this age in which science has outstripped man's abilities to cope with the conditions he has created; in which thought is increasingly dominated by science to the exclusion of faith …'.[8] (That was back in 1947. Well, faith seems to be newly attractive in our day – even though the traditional beliefs are not, and the exercise of faith uncertain of its object seems, to an observer, peculiarly empty.)

Like Professor Read, we can see something of ourselves from the standpoint of much earlier 'scientists' like those alchemists of his. But we cannot go on to approve our improvements upon them! Especially is this true in matters of faith.

When I first went to Boethius, for example, it was with deep reverence – because I had read that he had clearly opposed the Arian heresy (the Arians tried to simplify the profound truth about two natures in our Lord Jesus, by insisting that he was only human). Moreover, Boethius was imprisoned by his overlord, an Arian, sentenced, and ultimately clubbed to death in accordance with the sentence. I longed for his fellowship across the centuries. It did not trouble my initial awe to learn that there were political jockeyings between his overlord and the Eastern Emperor, between the Goths' supporters, and the Greek culture to the East; or that some historians saw Boethius as compromised in the political choices he made. What did disturb me was finding a good deal of Plotinus and not as obtrusively the evidence of Scripture in his text. When I looked up Plotinus, I read that he 'gave abiding shape to Neoplatonism'. And my dictionary said that Neoplatonism 'was the dominant philosophy of the pagan world from the mid-3rd century A.D. down to the closing of the pagan schools by Justinian in 529.' Now Boethius was executed in 524. His thought 'echoed Christian sentiments', said my dictionary. Was that all? Give up on reading him then? Or allow him to be a man for his time and try to find out how, across the centuries, to communicate with him?

Two rewards I remember, from pressing on. But first came his argument about what we call 'the problem of evil' (this bare argument was distinctly *not* the reward!). He said that (a) God is good, and (b) There is nothing He cannot do. Can God do evil then? No, being good He cannot. And since there is nothing He cannot do, therefore evil is nothing![9] Even before I had pondered the grief-stricken argument of *When Bad Things Happen to Good People*,[10] just on the basis of my own experience, this argument of Boethius's chilled me with its brainy emptiness. And then I remembered that the *Consolation* was written while Boethius was on death row. It was humbling – maybe he had to be a little specious, to work on, under those circumstances!

The traces of Neoplatonism in a sixth-century man's thinking we may at first condemn, then indulge as we gain historical perspective. But do we glimpse how we may look from the vantage-point of another culture far removed from ours? The point here is, how infiltrated we can be by the very air of the world around us. How hard it is to be in the world but not of it (to paraphrase our Lord's words in John 17:13–18). How carefully we must listen to all clues that may help us diagnose the blind spots we have contracted·from the illness of our particular culture, at least as easily as we see and condemn the bad spots in another's, long ago. This degree of watchfulness may become obsessive; also, it may fail, unless someone from outside spots the blind spots, the way an outsider hears our accents.

Does the very curriculum of our secular universities (and of the Christian universities that also give accredited degrees) help or hinder us in knowing ourselves? Heal or further infect us? But we are of our time, not outside it; we are in the miasma of this violent, headlong, desperate, fragmenting world. The salt that checks corruption has to be rubbed against the corruptible. And the salt is not ourselves, except as Jesus Christ presences Himself, in mercy, even in us, even here and now. We may not know when this happens. It is certainly not in our power to make it happen. We are all, alike, in His hands, in or of the world though we be. 'Be comforted;' Pascal writes, 'it is not from yourself that you must expect it, but on the contrary you must expect it by expecting nothing from yourself.'[11] (He does not unriddle the 'it'.)

The more we listen to each other across the seeming barriers – different times, seemingly opposed positions like science and faith – the more our categories and distinctions dwindle, if a search for God's truth is our concern.

Back to Boethius and my two rewards – the second I am saving for tomorrow night, but it registered as far truer than a mere 'echo of Christian sentiments'. Boethius's *Consolation* contains a startling statement – this was in the sixth century: 'As we have shown, every object of knowledge is known not as a result of its own nature, but of the nature of those who comprehend it....'[12] Is that very different from the twentieth century's Heisenberg principle (willing to doubt the veracity of the observed because the observer's presence is an inevitable part of the process and may screen or skew what is seen)?

Once I was browsing in a periodical room, picking up anything that did not deal with English literature, and chanced upon a piece I could not follow, not far; but it was readable enough to refresh my stale mind. It was a speculative article. The scientist dealt with physics, but used more words than symbols – which was what had attracted me. 'It is a question whether the universe is isomorphic with mathematics,' he said. I can't remember who he is. I can't remember the rest of the article. But in all these years I have not been able to forget his sentence. He held that mathematics is the preferred language of advanced science because it is logical, airtight as it were. No wonder. Mathematicians, scientists, invented that language. It fits our reason.

In everyday, received languages, as one linguist put it, 'all grammars leak'; they lack ultimate precision, much of the vocabulary being poetry, i.e. metaphor, stained with history and faraway cultures. (The Bible was that linguist's central topic; I am sorely tempted to digress, so beautiful was his glimpse of the Eternal One. As Genesis records, God spoke a word – 'Let there be' – and it was done. Nonetheless He longed for relationship with us humans that would be free on both sides, and to that end He had to accommodate Himself to our limitations. For Him, speaking with us meant 'lisping in our language', just as He, once for all, limited Himself to all the conditions of our mortality.) The point here is that in words the user, the generator, distorts by being the framer, and for the sake of the receiver's understanding, far more than Heisenberg's observer may distort in his disciplined act of observing. Yet if scientists are beginning to question their own range and objectivity, who am I to dispute with them?

Wasn't it Jacques Ellul who declared that the devil in the twentieth century has been Efficiency? Certainly the old assurance that we make general progress as science progresses is no more. There is nothing today to compare with the heady excitement Englishmen felt at the time the Royal Society was established, the time when Coleridge attended Davey's lectures and wrote enthusiastic, full reports, the time when Darwin classed himself as an amateur. Is even space travel a mark of progress to us now? Or is it a panicky provision, a preparation for a time when we might need a life-raft to set ourselves afloat in the cold, cold universe – science's achievements having taught us how to blow up, burn out, or otherwise devastate this planet through social mismanagement? Those scientists who still earnestly seek to better the management need a manageable, contained community for their work, and where is it to be found? The doctors, e.g., who combat diseases and raise infant survival rates, begin to dread that over-population will do what bombs could do, only more gradually. This is not my view of our future, just what I think comes of the old view of 'progress' through science.

Ours is a disheartening era – a revolutionary time perhaps. The most hopeful see it that way. Its ambivalent drives, its sputterings and stallings, affect us all, and make a clear perspective hard to come by. Lest we grow disheartened by the climatic hazards and misunderstandings that beset us, as a society, we switch attention now to hazards we can work on, in the realistic hope of hearing better and understanding more clearly.

A person's climate exists, as well as society's, and it is a climate with emotional seasons and variations within seasons. We can learn to recognize what we feel. How does that help? Well, for example, through my forty-odd years of pre-Christian life, I had flinched at or detested certain words common in the Christian subculture (even into my early years, be it noted, the Christian subculture was the dominant one in this country). For example, 'evil' was such a word; 'abominable' and 'iniquity' were others. I said I 'detested' these and other words heard glibly through the years and never examined.

After I became a Christian, I set out to cope with the lingering repulsion by examining them one by one. 'Detest'? It turned out to be related to 'testimony': de- 'away from', i.e. a witness or testimony away from something. Detesting, it appeared, was in itself a way of misunderstanding! The next two words were 'evil' and 'iniquity', and if you hear 'equity' underlying 'iniquity' you have the clue. Iniquity is 'off balance'. The e- of 'evil', like ex-, is a negative prefix, and the -vil is related to the first syllable of 'balance' ('v' and 'b' sounds often bring the same word from one language to another; e.g. German's heben is the English word 'heave'). So 'evil', like 'iniquity', turned out to be a lurching off centre – compared with the equipoise of goodness. If evil seems livelier that too is evidently a misunderstanding. And it leads to inhumane behaviour, 'abominable' behaviour, i.e. ab- (in-) -homine (-humane)! So often the words I felt were repulsive turned out to have been twisted over the course of long usage; their original meaning explained them in ways I could accept.

The associations felt with some words often proved misleading as well. 'Righteous' was a word lost from my language at first; it was present only in the usage 'self-righteous' and carried that smell with it. But the *'right-'* part is, like the word *Recht* in German, a word of fairness. I chased the *–eous* part of the word around in my treasured *Etymological Dictionary* (Ernest Klein's, completed in North York, published by Elsevier in 1971 – and dedicated to his mother and father, his wife and only child, all of whom died in the concentration camps of the Second World War). It was a more devious trail than usual, but I think he was telling me that *–eous* is linked with both *wis* 'seeing, knowing', and *–os* (Greek) which means 'abounding in'. 'Righteous' then, is seeing and knowing clearly and abounding in fairness.

Out of consideration for you, I left until the end, tonight, these verbal tactics against misunderstanding; had I started at the outset we might have spent a whole evening with words and meanings of this kind! For instance, it seems wrong not to go on now to one more inverted meaning. The 'wicked' we tend to think of as the tough guys. But the root of 'wicked' is the same as that of 'weak' (the Germans have *weichen*, 'yield'), and it means 'soft'!

Isn't it instructive to see how centuries of human beings, like myself all those years, took over some key words, and gave them associations or overtones that in many instances put evil for good or good for evil? The rebels' central discard from this vocabulary, of course, is 'sin'. Klein derives it from the Latin for 'guilty', *sons*, and claims that the Latin word is probably a present participle from *sum, esse*, 'to be'. Even more helpful is a Concordance that groups Biblical words under the words in the original Hebrew and Greek. One Greek word, translated 'sin' in athletics or, metaphorically, in ethics, is the archer's term, 'missing the mark'. There is a common Hebrew word, also translated 'sin', that defined it in relation to the moral commandments of God.

Most rebels know they have no wish to break those parts of the moral law that have become civil law, e.g. murder or stealing, no wish to break them and risk being caught, at least. Lying is not such a clear matter to many persons. When refugees on the Nova Scotia coast landed with tales of many days at sea, but in dry clothing that belied the tales, there was a phone-in show on the radio, 'Should Canada accept these people even though they lied to the authorities?' Every single respondent on the air that day spoke to immigration issues of one kind or another, but the radio's man had to keep reminding them about the 'lies' part of his question. And every caller said, 'O well, yes, but they had to lie to cover the facts.' As if that were not the purpose of *any* lie! In our culture, we do not really know or respect the moral code given in the Bible however much we may deplore the lawlessness that seems to be taking over. Alister McGrath sees *lawlessness* as the prison: when Christ delivers a person, it is a jail-break out of lawlessness into freedom.

It is his assumption, and mine, that it is impossible either to be bored by or to reject Jesus Christ. 'But I *am* bored, and I *do* reject Christianity,' you may think. No. You are bored by or reject some notion of what it is, put off by somebody's notion who presents a blurred picture, or by a misunderstood idea from other people's ideas. It is a Person with whom you will have to do, and He is not boring; seen clearly, He could not be rejected. Jesus is consistent with all the difficult-to-accept disciplines and commands but in a new dimension; He is, as it were, God translating Himself into the language of our kind of being, so that we can understand and, in Him, want the goodness of those disciplines and commands.

Evade Him we can, and it can seem the less dangerous course. I knew a child through all her growing-up who became a university scholar; she kept lending me books like Castaneda on peyote-visions, or various rationalists' arguments; and I read in order to keep in contact. But finally I said, 'I have been reading your books off and on for two years now. Isn't it about time you read my Book – at least one of the Gospels in it?' Her answer, after a minute, was as honest as all her thinking: 'Margaret,' she said, 'I'm afraid to.' She is right. The greatest danger is to stop evading. Unless you consider it damaging to grow.

Notes

1. Cardinal (John Henry) Newman, *The Idea of a University*, ed., with Introduction and Notes by I. T. Ker (Oxford: Clarendon Press, 1976), 255, 256.

2. Newman, 255.

3. *Every End Exposed: the 100 Koans of Master Kido with the Answers of Hakuin-Zen*, trans. and commentary by Yoel Hoffmann (Brookline, Mass.: Autumn Press, 1977), 20.

4. E. M. W. Tillyard, *Studies in Milton* (London: Chatto & Windus, 1951), 138.

5. Tillyard, 138.

6. Tillyard, 139.

7. H. Butterfield, *Origins of Modern Science* (1949) (as cited in Tillyard, p. 139).

8. John Read, *The Alchemist in Life, Literature and Art* (London: Thomas Nelson & Son, 1947), 2, 2, 1, 2.

9. Boethius, *The Consolation of Philosophy*, trans., with an introduction by V. E. Watts (Harmondsworth: Penguin, 1969), III, 12, 113.

10. Rabbi Harold S. Kushner, *When Bad Things Happen to Good People* (New York: Schocken Books, 1981). [The 'grief-stricken event' was the death of Kushner's young son at age 14 from 'progeria', premature aging.]

11. Blaise Pascal, *Pensées*, trans. A. J. Krailsheimer (1966), no. 202, 95. [In W. F. Trotter, trans., *Pensées/The Provincial Letters* (New York: Modern Library, 1941), no. 518, 'it' does not need to be unriddled: 'It is not from yourself that you should expect grace....' Ephesians 2:8 expresses it: 'For by grace you have been saved through faith, and that not of yourselves; it is the gift of God' (New King James Version). The passage in Pascal's original is 'Consolez-vous! Ce n'est pas de vous que vous devez l'attendre, mais au contraire, en n'attendant rien de vous, que vous devez l'attendre.' *Pensées*, texte établi par Léon Brunschvicg (Paris: Garnier-Flammarion, 1976), no. 517. The key word in no. 516 being *foi*, perhaps 'faith' would be a slightly more accurate English word than 'grace', though the two words are interrelated in the New Testament.]

12. Boethius, vol. 6, 163.

LECTURE TWO:

UNDERSTANDING

IS COSTLY

PREAMBLE TO THE PROPOSITIONS

I am not qualified to pontificate about either the university or Christianity. But both are places of learning, and therefore the focus tonight will be 'understanding'.

All data are neutral. It's in the selecting and interpreting – and the emphasis fashionable in any given time – that 'understanding' becomes muddied.

No one is without bias. Everyone has a counter-Christian bias or a Christian bias, at any given stage of life, in any given circumstance.

What, then, is understanding? Who does understand?

Instead of logical order I again tonight follow propositional magneting of ideas.

PROPOSITIONS

Objective: understanding without compromise.

Alien doctrine, i.e. someone else's doctrine, grew in a different soil; something can be learned from anything or anybody who is alive and growing.

Conviction does not preclude listening.

Contention tends to defensiveness.

The true believer's problem: how to say 'I am here,' and still be saying 'I am not not-there.'[1]

UNDERSTANDING IS COSTLY

That last proposition is not a riddle. It points to a modifying one learns from the experience of heartfelt sympathy. There can be a drift into 'I am here – and I am there', which is a very different statement. It is all very well to 'walk a mile in his or her moccasins', but that is not knowing what it is to *be* him or her. As a reviewer commented, in an article on John Howard Griffin's *Black Like Me*, it's one thing for a white man to make his skin colour dark and thus learn about racial discrimination first-hand. But he is still a white man; he is shaped by the acceptance, encouragement, opportunities, he knew in childhood. He can never know the receptor-sensitivities of the man born to dark racial memories and raised in a black ghetto, actual or invisible.

Trying to be 'there' rather than 'not not-there' had relevance to students, in the days when I taught on a campus. Some of the good readers had a bad time exercising what Keats called 'negative capability' – that human openness 'that Shakespeare had so enormously'. A watercolourist must be highly skilled to control whether, or how, the colours will run into each other. Comparable care is needed in exercising this faculty of receptiveness. Students can suffer stress, if they identify with Nietzsche while studying him in philosophy, and then with Marie Curie in the science course, and so on. A committed Christian too can 'love his neighbours' in the same mistaken way. As an example, an excellent way to begin working in the inner city is to spend a morning in the application-queue at a welfare office. But to confuse a deepening sympathy with *really* knowing what it is like to be 'there' is to drift towards determinist attitudes that rob the poor of the dignity of moral responsibility, 'explaining' everything and anything as caused by their hardships and family troubles. (There is one intriguing way of defining original sin: Adam and Eve had no parents to blame!)

No, if we are *here*, we cannot genuinely be 'there' as well. But we can hope to be 'not not-there'. An instance of the attempt is recorded in Harry Blamires' *The Christian Mind*. He describes 'one feature of our intellectual life' as being 'a living dialogue' between writers past and present and readers in the same culture. Writing in 1963, he reported the best writing to be non-Christian – Samuel Beckett's, for instance. Puritans (Blamires' term) have remarked that Beckett's novels and plays have been called obscene. But 'nowhere more poignantly are we searched out and known,' Blamires insists. Such writing is 'profound and penetrating. This represents a deep and wholly human response to present-day life.' Yet 'there is no current Christian dialogue on this topic ... no Christian conversation which I can enter, bringing this topic or this vision with me.... The thinking Christian who is concerned over these issues finds himself fitfully and perversely ... out of touch with his fellow-Christians.'[2]

He is aware of being 'here' as a Christian, but not 'not-there' when he reads Beckett! The understanding is clearly painful. More of us need to come to it. I wish universities and churches were effective in stimulating Christian students to a like experience. In truth, there is no place, either in ivory tower or in comfortable pew, for our troubled adventuring.

Like all new understandings, this kind highlights a need for more understanding. May that 'living dialogue' be recovered on a new level? For example, it is impossible for us, in natural terms, to believe in the transforming of a skid-row derelict, or a modern-day persecuting Saul. In supernatural terms it *is* believable. What Blamires has called 'the living dialogue' of a homogeneous culture is gone. But what broke through our communication barrier we cannot understand, we only witness! 'The poet's job,' according to Mégroz, is 'to prove that we are wiser than we know.... Philosophy, science and morality are essentially empirical; poetry ... and religion necessarily transcend and anticipate demonstrable experience and therefore cannot be *fully* expressed or understood rationally.'[3] (The italics are mine.) Our wisdom waits – in the wings! Blamires is English – and a university professor, which is different from being a Canadian or American and a professor, especially from being a professor at Oxford where church and university are so much one that Cardinal Newman felt obliged to leave a senior post at Oxford when his convictions led him away from the Anglican into the Roman Catholic Church.

Echoes of past events survive in England; stray evidences of tradition are tolerated, even embraced. We think of Iris Murdoch as primarily a novelist, but in 1970 she published *The Sovereignty of Good,* and in 1992 *Metaphysics as a Guide to Morals.* True, she writes that 'there is, in my view, no God in the traditional sense of the term,' and with humility and honesty she adds 'and the traditional sense is probably the only sense.'[4] Again, she concedes that we are struggling today to entertain, 'in a way that is not false ...', the notion that 'it all somehow must make sense.'[5] She has been a professor of metaphysics at Oxford, as well as a novelist. And Blamires is a Christian apologist as well as an English professor.

Either one would be unlikely to hold senior posts on this continent – unless at a Christian-academic institution, or unless their public performance remained academic. This is not to say that England is less secular than North America, as a society, only that traditions and points of defensiveness differ. Incidentally, the Englishman Blamires, unlike most of us Canadians, is consistently careful to distinguish 'secular' (the statement of fact, for example the secular, not the cloistered, clergy), from 'secularist' (a value system with its own missionary zeal). Yet both he and Iris Murdoch, speaking for their society, probably speak for North American society too. It is a step of understanding to name one's present place of being – however bleak. But alas, there is danger: of saying 'Here I stand!' in glum self-congratulation which can imply that any less bleak place is dishonest (hypocritical). That would be a misunderstanding, both of oneself and of the issues.

Is an open question-mark, sometimes, a waiting way of moving ahead? Speculation can push a person on to active research, can it not?

But to make a move – as many scientists will attest – takes careful planning. There is a cost. Facing it, and risking the next step all the same, is painful.

Everyone flashes some image of pain on his inner screen, drawn from TV or memory or from the sharp pictures imagination forms reading Amnesty International literature, perhaps, or from reading the daily paper. But – I am quoting now – 'the worst pain of all is to see the knife pass into your flesh, and to feel nothing.' I *think* that is Unamuno, but it may be Ortega y Gasset; it is someone I absorbed in the flow of reading half a century ago. Pain, loss, is defined as a beginning-point in the Gospels. You must spend all, i.e. lose all, to gain more than all, qualitatively speaking. Love defined himself ('God is love') by total loss – of privacy, of reputation, of friends, of all freedom and all rights, loss of physical life and of any supernatural rescue – even of any hope of rescue. It was deliberate. The stranger truth, even: He wants us to share this loss, for love's sake. Erma Bombeck clarifies this meaning for us. It may be in a pop arts voice, an Americanized voice, but hear her.

When the good Lord was creating mothers, He was into His sixth day of overtime when the angel appeared and said, 'You're doing a lot of fiddling around on this one!'

The Lord said, 'Have you read the specs on this order?

'She has to be completely washable, but not plastic;

'Have 180 moveable parts … all replaceable;

'Run on black coffee and leftovers;

'Have a lap which disappears when she stands up;

'A kiss that can cure anything from a broken leg to a disappointed love affair;

'And six pairs of hands.'

The angel shook her head slowly and said, 'Six pairs of hands? No way.'

'It's not the hands that are causing me problems,' said the Lord. 'It's the three pairs of eyes that mothers have to have.'

'That's on the standard model?' asked the angel.

The Lord nodded. 'One pair that sees through closed doors when she asks "What are you doing in there?" when she already knows.

'Another here in the back of her head that sees what she shouldn't but what she has to know, and of course the ones here in front that can look at a child when he goofs up and say, "I understand and I love you," without so much as uttering a word.'

'Lord,' said the angel, touching his sleeve gently, 'come to bed. Tomorrow –'

'I can't,' said the Lord. 'I'm so close to creating something so close to myself. Already I have one who heals herself when she is sick ... can feed a family of seven on one pound of hamburger ... and can get a nine-year-old to stand under a shower.'

The angel circled the model of a mother very slowly and sighed. 'It's too ... soft.'

'But tough!' said the Lord excitedly. 'You cannot imagine what this mother can do or endure.'

'Can it think?'

'Not only think, but it can reason and compromise,' said the Creator.

Finally the angel bent over and ran her finger across the cheek.

'There's a leak,' she pronounced. 'I told you that you were trying to put too much into this model.'

'It's not a leak,' said the Lord, 'it's a tear.'

'What it is for?'

'It's for joy, sadness, disappointment, pain and loneliness and pride.'

'You are a genius,' said the angel.

The Lord looked somber. 'I didn't put it there.'

Again I hoarded this composition for years – and have forgotten its source.[6] This is a good place to confess the jackdaw process that underlies what I say. So many people stimulate a thought, or speak a memorable word, and their faces, their names, fade in the course of time. Or I do remember and don't want to pause at every comma to provide the credit due.

Here is one credit, now, for an idea applicable throughout both lectures, which it would be a pleasure to provide. My Grandmother Kirkland had this saying: 'My girl, you can learn something from everybody. Something to do. Or something not to do.' She died in 1928 but her sagacity has proved unfading.

The vulnerable reader of literature learns to suspend judgement, in order to listen well. Consider *The Cruising Auk*, a sequence by George Johnston. In one of its poems, 'After Thunder', a city-man notices the fresh earth smell, 'the ecstatic air/after the passion and flood of August rain' – an overwhelming 'careless pleasure' that only the birds dare utter, but their voicing 'pierces us: the ecstatic edge of pain'. In the poem 'Rain', the sequence has moved on to a darker season, and, in place of exhilaration, now there is enervation ('I'd rather never have been born/ than feel the way I do again'). In Part Two there are several portraits, incisively but uncompromisingly drawn (would we all not choose, secretly at least, to have an artist compromise a little in presenting us?). But Part Three closes with an amused cherishing of the old earth, all the more for its 'slightly wobbling spin' and for its indifference to us and to our questing ('My why and how are me'). The quiet coming to terms with experience strips down to that enigmatic self-definition. And at the very end comes a coda, an acid observation of the seasons of mortal awareness, annually, and the synchronized appearing of tax forms and mail order catalogues that give 'mortality the lie'.[7]

It would be a crass impertinence to the poem's truth to misread the 'why and how' as questions *we* might be able to answer. That would be misunderstanding, with the damage attached: we would cut off communication between ourselves and the poem, losing it and impoverishing ourselves. There is wise understanding in the sequence that always, implicitly, accepts the ambiguous. We have to stretch ourselves to 'see' this way as we listen. It is one kind of truth, experienced through the words. No wonder George Johnston was drawn to the dark glimmering old Norse sagas. I wish he were here reading them to us right now.

But all this mirroring of Everyman's adaptations over his decades does nothing to diminish, indeed it anchors, a perfect little poem in Johnston's *Home Free* sequence. Clear in understanding, it is heartbroken and heartbreakingly beautiful, personal as well as timelessly valid wherever what he calls 'unspoiled' has brought anyone to his knees. Look it up. The title is 'No Way Out.'[8]

Rarely is an act or utterance so authentic that one is stilled by it – far past the ugly stage of 'understanding' that reacts to goodness with guilt, i.e. with vanity. 'No Way Out' shares that authenticity with an occurrence I witnessed in a freshman English seminar one late November morning. The facts I can outline; the event will escape –

words and data cannot communicate pure event. We had gathered. Some student probably had a report to present. We all had books and notebooks. There was the usual shuffle of latecomers settling in, questions left over from last week being cleared up. And in the pause before the day's report began, one of the young men stood up and spoke, forcefully, in his usual quiet way, but very close to tears. (He was a great reader, new in Toronto, down from northern Ontario, and his presence in the group had been a pleasure to us.) What he said to us was, 'Do you realize that this year's first snow has begun to fall? And nobody noticed at all?' The large window gave on a cement ledge, and part of the building's grey wall, and a few flakes of snow were whirling lazily and touching down, not melting. We all looked. 'I can't stay here,' the young man said, gathering up his books. He walked out of that seminar and out of the college. He did not return. But I think we all hoped that the receptiveness he had nurtured in himself found ways of developing in whatever new context he sought out for himself. The effect of that indelible event was, oddly, one of hope. A glimpse of some understanding that enveloped the pain, costly, but in a positive dynamic.

Hope is not lightly come by. The cruel person, for example, may be transformed, one here, one there. 'Evil must not be let flourish' as an embattled and pugnacious friend said recently. Yet Petra Kelly, the Green Party's leader, has been murdered,[9] with the evil she identified flourishing as she went under. Or one becomes aware of a familiar street person, solitary, gaunt, muttering to himself, 'coping in the community', as it is urbanely called.

May Sarton has an unusual book, *As We Are Now*, purportedly the journal of a woman in her seventies. She had been committed to a remote nursing home that the inspectors hadn't yet caught up with, the care her frail health demanded not being possible in the home of an even older and frailer brother and his overtaxed wife. During the early days she longed to see her brother, knowing he would be brought to visit, not knowing how soon. During this period she was 'sick with fear and disgust. And in a strange way, I still had hope.' Finally the brother did visit. But after she had anticipated so long how good the visit would be, she found herself, seeing him, in tears; she could not stop crying, more and more uncontrollably. 'It was when hope left me after that visit,' she wrote, 'that I began the road back.... I am myself again. I know that I must expect no help from the outside. This is it. Here I stand.' Her fortress became cold, resolute anger.[10]

Ivan Illich said once that the 'survival of the human race depends on its rediscovery of hope as a social force.'[11] But hope disappointed turns into anger, as it did with the nursing home patient. The disruption Illich looked for has not brought us out into anything very promising, not yet. From a recent book review I gather that John Lukacs says the modern world has ended, that when Soviet Communism ended all of us were launched on a transition to the post-modern world. I have not read his book yet, but isn't there a glimmer of hope in the prospect? Times of transition before now have produced disruption – and excellence. The unsettling days of explorers and new commerce produced Shakespeare; the upheaval in the late Renaissance produced a split in the church, Jansenism – within Roman Catholicism, but without its seal of approval – the deepened spirituality reflected in Pascal's *Pensées*; the French Revolution and Napoleon were Beethoven's times.

The *–versity* part of *university* is the same word as the German *werden* ('become'). Where else is there a context so conducive to what I think of as the panoramic insights peculiar to the young? Students are at an age when life-energies peak wonderfully; they even provision the young to dare contemplating sadness in a way no adult will be able to afford, after experiences and memory have weighed in. There can never again be that wide-angle lens flooding one with brilliant pain and comprehension. The Germans call it *Weltschmerz*. It is a gift to the new generation, received, like every good thing, by anyone game to step across the threshold of fear into a unique, undefinable, yet very distinct kind of knowing.

The *uni-* part of *university*? Perhaps the process of synthesizing all we learn there? But around what magnet? Cardinal Newman would say that the focus comes by relating everything to God; or rather perceiving God through everything learned, discovering that He is everywhere and always seeking relation with us. (Incidentally, *focus*, my dictionary says, is simply the Latin word for 'hearth'.) We still speak of the *uni*verse, the whole, without losing in that wholeness one particle of the marvellous array of particulars, organic and inorganic, visible and invisible and well nigh untrackable. Learning, even in the world's terms, is vast; our capacities are limited and our time here very short. How can we catch the illimitable in our little bottles? Yet we must learn precision with particulars as well as spacious thinking across centuries. In practical terms we keep building connections between these extremes.

As an example, when I was an undergraduate the curriculum listed 'Philosophy 3c' and 'Philosophy 3c (St. Michael's)'. Roman Catholic students read different texts from different periods. Of course there was a legend: all of us having gathered in Exam Hall in May, and one flustered student being given the St. Michael's paper by mistake, scanning questions he could not even recognize from his studying – in some versions realizing in time to switch, in others flunking. A minority with a special focus selects different traditions, different topics of discussion. But university can train us to be aware of varied approaches. Today's University of Toronto plans for interactions, especially for theologs, among all the campus's colleges. Mutual receptiveness, whatever our particular standpoints, is a step towards understanding.

Oddly, the supposedly bigoted Christian is more likely to develop receptivity than the counter-Christian majority to subject matter each finds uncongenial. The Christian learns the world's ways as a survival tactic; whether or not he is generous in spirit, he cannot cut himself off altogether without losing his sanity and denying his faith. Shakespeare has a term we could appropriate here to clarify the meaning (as W.H. Auden did[12] in applying it to literary criticism):

... my nature is subdued to what it works in, like *the dyer's hand*.[13]

A Christian's obligation to absorb the other is both bane and blessing, all entangled as it is with both compromise and compassion.

But in what other field of study would so many people reach so dismissing conclusions, on the basis of so little knowledge, as outsiders are comfortable with in disregarding Christian truth? When I taught a Milton course, in the sixties, a delegation of freshmen came after class to say, 'In high school we had Greek myths twice and the primitive myths once, but we never took the Christian myths, and we need a quick survey of these in order to understand Milton.' Even people who had been taught Bible stories in childhood, even those who had been quickened by that learning, have usually taken little time for adult levels of Christian knowledge – so much else to do, so much else to absorb. The geographer from Oxford [Dr James M. Houston] who founded Regent College in Vancouver made it the objective of that Canadian school to help graduates upgrade their knowledge of the faith to the same level as their knowledge, theoretical and practical, of the sciences or humanities that had been their specialty.

We need all our minds and all our hearts and souls and strength (or bodily energies) – we need it all to – understand? to love, rather, when the object of our love is the One who is sole source of 'seeing', and of caring and doing and growing. It sounds strenuous. But 'nothing could preserve its own nature as well as go against God,'[14] wrote Boethius, early in the sixth century. The same truth is jubilantly celebrated in Psalm 148 where 'great sea creatures and all ocean depths ... do His bidding,' i.e. where this kind of cosmic delight is a by-product of simply being who we are made to be – *that* is His will, His bidding!

Another Boethius passage was promised in the first lecture, a little jewel: he is thinking about time. Even if, as in Aristotelean thought, the world had no beginning, and will have no end, nevertheless, he reasons, whatever has being in time has lost yesterday, and lacks everything future; endlessness, therefore, is not eternity, which includes past, present and future in its 'now'. 'Eternity then' (here is the jewel), 'is clearly the property of the mind of God. God ought not to be considered as older than the created world in extent of time, but rather in the immediacy of His nature.'[15] Worldly contenders for or against evolution will need the new faceting of a larger, revealed Reality, to hear the cogency of this observation.

We say we 'see', at moments of understanding. But we do not see with the multi-faceted eyes an insect brings to the act. Our limitations, once we acknowledge them, liberate us to steady plodding, and occasional awe.

One of Pascal's thoughts turns on an undefined 'it'. ('Be comforted; it is not from yourself that you must expect it,[16] but on the contrary you must expect it by expecting nothing from yourself.') (See page 28.)

Echoing the Psalmist, but in my own voice, I say – of the Lord, the one God of all people everywhere, '*My* God, *my* Jesus', just the way a two-year-old sitting on the front steps says to an approaching visitor, 'Are you coming to *my* house?' When people said things like that to me before I knew for myself what they were talking about, I was intrigued and exasperated. There is for a long time in one's search an impasse, a spiritual hunger which refuses, has been culturally conditioned to refuse, the steps necessary to appease itself. A system of interlocking doctrines, present in the Bible, sufficiently defines the truth of God for the least educated and for the most intelligent and well-schooled. We are all given enough to work on, and more than enough. If more were given than we could hope ever to put into our three-dimensional being and doing, we would be able to theorize, perhaps ... but we might forget what is essential. Since this Book is in our language, and part of our cultural inheritance, why is it kept so closed by so many of us, one wonders?

A psychology professor told a story about an experiment he tried with one small class. He hired someone to dress in a Black Bag, which enveloped him from the soles of his feet to the top of his head, in which he learned to walk and see (through a transparent slit). Just as the class was beginning, week after week, the Black Bag would walk in, take a chair, sit unmoving; and just before the end of the period it would quietly walk out again. The atmosphere stayed tense and uneasy in the room. Nobody dared to ask. Certainly nobody approached the Bag.

I forget what the application was in that course on psychology! But the picture of the unfamiliar, the strange and unexplained, in our

midst, is vivid. We all walk about in a cloud of our own comprehension, seeing what we already know everywhere we look, elaborating
what we grasp, and yet we know we are, marvellously, never quite cut
off from what is out there.

Misty gropings, at that point of awareness, will never be good
enough. The thumping moral assertions of wise Solomon will put
solid ground under our feet. In Proverbs he asserts a moral law as
coherent and objective and unfailingly applicable as the physical law
of gravity. The truth given in the Holy Word is a disciplined, but not a
manageable enterprise. One of our craftiest evasions is trying to man-
age it, working up by ourselves from the living Word a system we feel
sure will keep us on the rails all the way. But no system *we* work out
from the inexhaustible wisdom of the Word will do. Truth is final, but
our mortal grasp of it never can be final. The word of truth is living and
probes us continually as we live our days and nights. It is a Voice that
speaks, revealing truth: 'the sound of many waters', in one passage; 'a
still small voice' in another;[17] overpowering one moment, companion-
able as an aside the next. Some passages are familiar, we think? In the
needy moment, one of those threadbare phrases will become steel,
surgical steel.

Does this sound inward-looking, me-centred? It is not so in practice. The Lord is the central person, the Lord, Wisdom,[18] who was the
'craftsman at his side' in creation, the Lord who was 'filled with
delight day after day,/ rejoicing always in his presence,/in his whole
world/ and delighting in mankind'.[19] When you read on to the biogra-
phies of Jesus, moreover, the 'you' of the text is a plural pronoun in
most cases. We are 'members one of another',[20] and this book increasingly develops in us this precious awareness. On the radio recently a
Cree woman spoke of the help she had from Alcoholics Anonymous.
A spokesman for native people was master of ceremonies on this call-
in program, and he endorsed her plea that people see alcoholism as an
illness, but then he added, 'Pain is *communal* too.' Yes.

There is a poem by W.R. Rodgers that traces a twelve-month journey of the Magi – a course through promise and bewilderment to the
darkest hour, just after Jerusalem had disappointed their hopes, and

Herod had sounded unreliable. Their discouragement was heavy. And then – the star did lead to the Infant King, after all. The poem ends,

> Now Age and Innocence can meet,
> Now, now the circle is complete,
> The journey's done.
> Lord, Lord, how sweet![21]

Next came the painful part: that was the beginning of the *really* long journey!

The titles of these two lectures use everyday words in their everyday sense. Late last week I suddenly realized that I had never been curious about the background of these words. What an awesome phenomenon language is, an echo chamber of ancestral insights and of our human psyches. *Understanding*, or 'standing under', is, in more logical languages like Dutch or German (*verstehen*), 'stand in front of, where one can see.' *Misunderstanding*, then, is trying to get by, instead of coping, and leads one to walk a crooked mile! The words *damaging* and *damning* are from an identical root; the word *danger*, although different in derivation, was 'influenced' by the first two in its meaning, says my etymological dictionary. (The two root meanings were 'to cut off, divide', and 'to damage'.)

'Costly' understanding? Apparently 'cost' comes from the Latin *constare* 'to stand together' (both Klein and Oxford agree). The word 'constant' is from the same root. Does this relate to our sense of 'cost'? Oxford tries to explain by a Latin quotation: '*Hoc constat mihi tribus assibus*' ('this "stands me in" at three asses'); however the English idiom 'stands me in', though it relates 'stand' to 'cost', allows 'constancy' to fade, and tends to lose sight of the other party. Cost involves more than one. Cost goes on a long time. The statement 'understanding is costly' suggests an additional element of painfulness.

I expected *pain* to have roughly its modern medical sense, but if it has, the connection must be theological, for it is from the root *paenitas*, 'punishment', 'penalty'. When a sick man mockingly says, 'I'm paying for a misspent life,' he is etymologically exact. But theologically this tight individualistic logic is dead wrong. It leaves out the cost factor. Pain will not fit within the bounds of our reason, of our understanding – as each of us discovers first-hand in time; no theory will explain it to our honest satisfaction.

Have I spent two evenings to say that misunderstanding and understanding alike lead to damage and pain? But is that surprising, since our understanding is always partial, a step forward into another part of what we sometimes feel is a maze? It will never be our understanding or intelligence that will rescue us. Oddly, that is the shining hope.

Notes

1. [The editors have substituted the word 'still' for what reads, both in her typescript (held in Archives and Special Collections, University of Manitoba) and the first edition of *A Kind of Perseverance*, 'not be'. 'The true believer's problem: how to say "I am here," and not be saying "I am not not-there".' The proposition is complicated enough without a misprint tightening the knot. As was pointed out in the Introduction, the context is to be found in Margaret Avison's autobiography, which in fact takes its title from another version of the proposition, something Avison said in answer to a question at the 1963 Vancouver Poetry Conference:

    This question was put by a registrant: 'What makes a poet's language distinctive?' We all fell silent, trying to pin it down, then tried to answer. Not just affection for words, which is common to all good writers; not necessarily a matter of cadence, formal structures, rhythm. The answer that came to me, forced out of minutes of dismissing options, was new to me too: 'It is saying "I am here and not not-there"' (*I Am Here and Not Not-there: An Autobiography*, The Porcupine's Quill, 2009).]

2. Harry Blamires, *The Christian Mind* (1963), 6–11.

3. R.L. Mégroz, *Modern English Poetry* 1882–1932 (1933), 5–7. [Avison has cut the first part of this in such a way as to make it a slightly more direct statement than it is in Mégroz's text: 'The justifiable assertion that works of art cannot be

judged by moral or philosophical standards, and that the poet's job was not to preach but to prove that we are wiser than we know, was reinterpreted as a manifesto against conventional morality and indeed any kind of orthodoxy such as the spiritual authority of the Christian Church.']

4. Iris Murdoch, *The Sovereignty of Good* (1970), 79.

5. Murdoch, 57–8.

6. ['When God Created Mothers – May 12, 1974,' in *Forever Erma: Best-Loved Writing from America's Favorite Humorist* (Kansas City: Andrews and McMeel, 1996), 16–18. The passage doesn't appear in the draft of *A Kind of Perseverance* held in the Archives and Special Collections, University of Manitoba. To make room for it, and/or perhaps to avoid quoting disproportionately from one source, Avison cut out quotations from most of the George Johnston poems she cites.]

7. George Johnston, *Endeared by Dark: The Collected Poems* (1990), from 'The Cruising Auk': 19, l. 22, *O Earth Turn*, 67, 68.

8. George Johnston, 106.

9. *New York Times*, Oct. 21, 1992.

10. May Sarton, *As We Are Now* (1973), 27, 35.

11. Ivan Illich, *Deschooling Society* (1970), 106.

12. W.H. Auden, *The Dyer's Hand* (1948).

13. Shakespeare, Sonnet CXI.

14. Boethius, III.12, 111.

15. Boethius, V.6, 164.

16. Blaise Pascal, *Pensées*, trans. A.J. Krailsheimer (1966), 202, 95.

17. Bible, New King James Version, Ezekiel 43:2; I Kings 19:12.

18. See Proverbs 8.

19. Bible, New International Version, Proverbs 8:30.

20. Bible, King James Version, Romans 12:5.

21. W.R. Rodgers, from 'The Journey of the Magi,' *Collected Poems* (1971), 119.

Photograph courtesy of *Kitchener-Waterloo Record*
Photographic Negative Collection, University of Waterloo Library.

MARGARET AVISON

Margaret Avison, widely admired for her richly dense and demanding poetry, was born in Galt (Cambridge) Ontario in 1918 and died in Toronto in 2007. Her post-secondary education was at Victoria College, the University of Toronto, though she attended a summer session at Indiana University and in 1956 held a Guggenheim Fellowship in Chicago, where she prepared the text of her first book, *Winter Sun*. Her early poetry had been included in important anthologies like A.J.M.Smith's landmark 1943 *The Book of Canadian Poetry*. Avison taught for two years at the University of Toronto's Scarborough College, and spent a year as writer-in-residence at the University of Western Ontario, but she never felt entirely comfortable in the academic context. In fact, she had a lifelong resistance to becoming established in *any* sort of career, feeling that to be so caught up would hinder the pursuit of her true vocation, poetry. She did work for several years at temporary jobs, mainly secretarial, some freelance.

Winter Sun (1960), a difficult and introspective but deeply compelling work, won the Governor General's Award for poetry. It was followed by *The Dumbfounding*, much of which issued from her 1963 Christian conversion and which introduced the new religious orientation of much of her poetry, which was to continue in other books like *sunblue* and *No Time*, winner of the 1990 Governor General's Award. Her 2002 collection, *Concrete and Wild Carrot*, was awarded the prestigious Griffin Poetry Prize. It was followed by two more collections, the last of which, *Listening*, appeared posthumously.

Margaret Avison's collected poems up to and including 2002 have been published in a three-volume set entitled *Always Now*. In 2009, her autobiography, *I Am Here and Not Not-There* was posthumously published.

In addition to her poetry prizes, Margaret Avison received three honorary doctorates, was made an Officer of the Order of Canada, and was the recipient of the Leslie K. Tarr Award for her outstanding contribution to Christian writing and publishing in Canada.